MEMORY

An Essay

By

WILLIAM LYON PHELPS

First published in 1929

British Library Cataloguing-in-Publication Data
A catalogue record for this book is available
from the British Library

William Lyon Phelps

William Lyon Phelps was born on 2nd January 1865, in New Haven, Conneticut, United States.

Phelps earned a B.A. in 1887, writing his thesis on the Idealism of George Berkeley.

He then gained an M.A. in 1891 from Yale and his PhD from Harvard in the same year. During his time a Yale, he offered a course in modern novels which brought the university considerable attention both nationally and internationally. This was quite controversial at the time and Phelps was pressured to give up the course, but eventually, due to popular demand, reinstated it outside the official curriculum.

In 1892, Phelps married Annabel Hubbard, sister of childhood friend Frank Hubbard, and the couple moved to the family estate overlooking Lake Huron. Phelps christened it "The House of the Seven Gables", after the Nathanial Hawthorne story of the same name.

He became a very popular figure at Yale but also as an inspirational orator. He went on lecture tours that drew large audiences, speaking on the virtues of modern literature.

He also preached regularly at the Huron City Methodist Episcopal Church and attracted such large crowds that the church was remodelled twice in five years to accommodate them.

Phelps published many essays on modern and European literature, including titles such as *Essays on Modern Novelists* (1910), *Some Makers of American Literature* (1923), and *As I Like it* (1923).

After his retirement from Yale in 1933, after 41 years of service, Phelps continued his public speaking, preaching, and writing a newspaper column. He also sat on book selection committees and acted as a judge for the Pulitzer Prize for literature.

His wife, Annabel, died from a stroke in 1939 and Phelps died four years later, in 1943.

MEMORY

I

THIRTY YEARS AGO I WAS standing near the eighteenth green of a golf course, watching the various contestants finishing in a tournament. I was particularly interested in the fate of an intimate friend, and as he and his antagonist approached the last cup, it appeared that they were exactly even. Owing to that peculiar curse of humanity, which makes it the more difficult to do anything in precise proportion to the strength of the desire to do it, my friend missed an absurdly easy putt, and was in consequence defeated. As he walked disconsolately toward the Club House, I murmured a word of conventional sympathy. "Oh," said he, "I don't mind so much now; the worst time is coming tonight, after I have gone to bed." He foresaw a whole night of sleepless torture, when he would play that miserable shot again and again. For just as it is sweet to recall a success and give it encore after encore in the mind, so the bitterest core of failure is its repetition in remembrance. The evil that we do would be comparatively easy to endure if we could do it only once. But we repeat it to the limit of exhaustion. Memory can be a torment as well as a comfort.

Some strangely-gifted individuals have a kink in the brain that gives them a freak memory, with which they can play tricks that seem almost miraculous. The well-beloved Ripley, whose

7

collection of human curiosities is exhibited in that diverting volume, Believe It or Not, informs us that the philosopher Seneca, upon listening attentively to a recital of two thousand disconnected words, could repeat them accurately in the order in which they had been spoken.

Lord Macaulay, after hearing a long oration, could repeat every word of it, as if he were reading it. Indeed he was reading it, reading it off the scroll of his brain. For his brain was like a sensitive plate, which recorded faithfully every sound it received.

Inasmuch as, so far as I know, the gift is unique, it may not be an impertinence to record the fact that my brother, the Reverend Doctor Dryden William Phelps, can recall some particular thing that has happened on any day during the last sixty years; and he can recall it immediately, upon demand, in response to any challenge. First of all, he possesses a talent so unusual that it has, in the case of other persons, been their sole source of income. Visiting on one occasion a dime museum, I found among the performers a man whose task was confined entirely to the following accomplishment. if you told him the date of your birth without mentioning the day he would, by calculations on a blackboard, in five minutes state the proper day of the week. For example:

I told him I was born on the second of January, 1865. After some figuring with the chalk on the board, he said confidently "Monday," which is correct. Yet my brother, with no paper, board, or figures, tells you that almost instantly by lightning mental arithmetic.

But his unique gift of memory is this. If you ask "What happened on March sixth, 1879?" or any other date within the last sixty years that you choose, in a few moments he will state the day of the week. Then he will give you the weather for that day, and describe some particular thing that happened. I have seen him tested many times, and have never known him to fail.

That eminent divine of the seventeenth century, the Reverend Doctor Thomas Fuller, author of a storehouse of anecdotes called

The Worthies of England, delighted in the display of his powers and in the invariable wonder of witnesses. He would be taken along a crowded thoroughfare in London, and after walking one hundred yards or so, would then repeat in the proper order all the signs of the shops on both sides of the street. He had an ocular, as Macaulay had an auricular, memory.

I have always believed that those who seem to possess a natural gift for correct spelling, really have the gift of an ocular memory. For on the rare occasions when they are in doubt -is it gauge or gauge-by writing the two forms, the memory instantly settles the matter. Correct spelling is by no means dependent on wide reading or on the ability to compose; Stevenson was a prodigious reader and an elegant writer, but he never could spell.

It was that same witty clergyman, Tom Fuller, who, anticipating the modern psychological attempts to localise brain functions, suggested that memory must be situated in the back of the head, because whenever anyone struggled to remember a particular date or event, he usually scratched there.

It is fatal to pretend to remember something that we have forgotten; it is much better to confess the humiliating truth, unless possibly one is so resourceful a diplomat as to be able to extricate oneself neatly from any trap. Such a fortunate man was accosted by a lady of some importance at a distinguished social function. He saw her coming toward him and he could not remember her name. "Ah," said she, "you don't remember me!" "Madame, for four years I have been trying in vain to forget you."

The downright cash payment of truth is better than the deferred and accumulating debt of falsehood. At dinner a wife asked that oft-heard question of her husband. Had he posted that letter she had given him at breakfast? "Yes, indeed," said he volubly: "I was so afraid I might forget it I carried it in my hand all the way to the letter-box, and dropped it in myself." "I didn't give you any letter this morning," said she.

We are all so vain that we love to have our names remembered by those who have met us only once. We exaggerate the talents

9

and virtues of those who can do this, and we are ready to repay their powers with lifelong devotion. The ability to associate in the mind names and faces is a tremendous asset to a politician; and it will prolong the pastorate of any clergyman. The late James G. Blaine was in this manner marvellously endowed, and he had unquestionably developed his powers by concentration. During his reign as Speaker of the House of Representatives at Washington, and on an occasion when he was presiding over a particularly turbulent debate, he was called out into the lobby to meet a dozen of his Maine constituents who had come to Washington to shake hands with him. He had never seen them before; but after a few moments of conversation, in which he spoke exactly the right word to each individual, he said goodbye; and as he shook hands with each pilgrim, he called him by his name. They departed, hoping they might soon have an opportunity to die for him.

President Eliot told me that in early life he had no gift at all for remembering the names of casual visitors; but believing it to be an important feature of the day's work, he had systematically cultivated his memory. Whenever he was introduced to a stranger, he looked earnestly at him, taking a mental impression of his face. Then while still regarding him, he repeated in his mind half a dozen times the stranger's name.

The well-known amiability of Americans-for we are beyond doubt the most amiable people in the world -makes us either tell lies or apologise where we ought to tell the truth and be unashamed. This especially applies to American women; they might profitably learn from the apparent rudeness of their British sisters. If a stranger asks the average American woman if she has read a certain novel, and it happens she has not and indeed possibly has never heard of it, she either lies and says she has, or else looks convicted of sin and regrets that she has not yet read that particular book. But if you ask an English woman if she has read a certain novel, she replies "Certainly NOT!" thus telling the truth, maintaining her superiority, and putting the questioner in the wrong.

There are worthy but unlucky saints who cannot remember anything. The champion of after-dinner speakers and one who survived all his listeners, was Chauncey M. Depew. He was asked by a beginner in the art if it was safe to tell a certain story; was it too old? Mr. Depew replied that at any dinner it was safe to tell any story, regardless of its age; "for at every dinner there is sure to be one person who has never heard anything."

In Gorki's famous tragedy, The Night Asylum, there is a decayed actor whose devotion to alcohol has destroyed his memory; and he is so grieved at this defect that he decides to hang himself. With the rope around his neck, he begins the Lord's Prayer, and finds that he cannot remember it. Thus he dies with an ultimate failure. Another person, however, though similarly affected, considered it more lightly. "There are three things I never can remember first, I can't remember faces; second, I can't remember names; and-and -I've forgotten what the third thing is I can't remember."

It is perhaps excusable that we are pleased when others remember our names; for the name is the only thing standing between an individual and absolute oblivion. When a mother decides to call her child Elizabeth or Frank, she is labelling that human being for time and eternity. It is the only passport to remembrance. What's in a name? Everything.

II

ALTHOUGH THE MAJORITY of persons who are blessed with active and original minds have in addition an excellent memory, the two do not invariably combine. There are individuals with remarkable power of cerebration whose memory is not extraordinary. It is rather a pity that in school and college education so much stress is placed on mere remembrance and so little on initiative and original thought. Examinations and so-called intelligence tests usually reveal only the candidate's ability to remember what he has read or heard. They do not always uncover his power of thinking; seldom his originality.

Still, in all courses in literature, nothing is better for the pupil than to have his mind filled with great poetry, great prose, and great ideas. It is better for the average student to know much of Shakespeare by heart than it is to devote himself to problems of authorship, interpolations or textual criticism. In my courses in Shakespeare, I not only permit, but encourage undergraduates to substitute for answers to the examination questions, passages from the poet accurately remembered.

It is better to have the mind furnished with the language of Shakespeare than with the crude thoughts of its possessor; just as it is better to have a house furnished with Chippendale chairs than with those made by the proprietor, no matter how industrious and painstaking he may be.

The memory is like a bank. The capital coin deposited is not only safe, but bears interest, yields dividends that accumulate with time. Thus a mind stored with elevating thoughts and ideas expressed in beautiful language is perhaps better than a strong-box filled with cash. Great ideas, exquisite phrases, are something more than good mental furniture. They yield dividends, which, though intangible and imponderable, may be of more personal enrichment than money.

Cultivez votre jardin. The memory is like a garden. Flowers and fruits and vegetables come with care; weeds come with carelessness. If one plants in the garden the right seeds and devotes constant vigilance and affectionate effort to their cultivation, the result will be either beautiful or useful or both. Thus if we plant in the mind inspiring ideas and the words of Writers of genius, we shall obtain results of permanent value.

If one goes to the theatre and sees a great play, the chief happiness comes long after the final curtain has fallen; it comes from remembrance and the stimulation of ideas. If one listens to the music of Beethoven, the mind is furnished with marvellous melodies that may be heard at any time in the meditation of remembrance. Conversely, tawdry motion pictures and cheap music fill the mind with dust and ashes. An orchard should produce fruit, not garbage.

Just as some houses are empty and some are crowded with things that positively hurt the eyes, so some minds are barren and hollow; their owners cannot live in them, but spend their lives seeking a way, any way of escape from themselves. Other minds are filled with "novelties," the "latest things," which make their owners undesirable company for the judicious.

Thus I maintain that whenever it is possible, the mind should be stored in early youth with the right things, the things that are lovely and of good report. Young people, young men and women, should, whenever it is possible, have the advantages of foreign travel. For the best part of foreign travel, like the best part of a good play, good music, good pictures, good books, is after the mind has received the first impact. Then remains that enormous balance in the bank of memory, which can be drawn upon at any time.

Certainly in foreign travel the best part is after one has returned home. By some fortunate freak of memory, the discomforts and misadventures of travel fade out of the picture;

the dross vanishes, and the gold remains.

Leave the fire ashes, what survives is gold. The reason why foreign travel should be indulged in by youth is twofold; they have all the later years to remember it, and the vigour and resilience of youth take discomfort and exposure as a jest. When one is old, one may be more able to appreciate the wonders of Europe; but one also has indigestion, one is easily fatigued, one cannot endure exposure. For while Europe contains far more things worth seeing than can be found in America, the United States of America is the only comfortable country in the world. No American over fifty is ever comfortable anywhere in Europe except in normal summer weather. When Thomas Carlyle was invited by a young friend to be his guest on a Continental journey, he declined with the remark, "You must remember that what is sport to you is death to me."

Merely to rid the mind of trivialities and vulgarities is not enough; we know what happened to the mind that was empty, swept, and garnished. Evil must be supplanted by good, and its place fully occupied. Why are "bad books," unclean plays, and suggestive pictures dangerous? There are many middle-aged men and women who believe that while these things do not hurt them, they will injure other people, especially youth. Now it is not necessary to worry about young people; for bad books, bad plays, bad pictures injure every man and woman, young and old, except those who are hopelessly ill. A man dying of cancer of the throat caused by smoking is, during the last stages of the disease, permitted to smoke. Why not? All healthy and normal men and women, no matter how old or experienced, are injured by immoral books; because these books, by filling the memory with sensual imagery, obscure the clear sky of the mind and dull the power of reason. It is, even under the most favourable circumstances, difficult in a world like this to live the life of reason; to keep a razor edge on perception and understanding. Everything that St. Paul called "fleshly lusts" dims the clear light of the mind and befogs the memory with miasma. There is absolutely no doubt about this, so, instead of worrying about the possible effects of these influences on minds younger and weaker, than ours, suppose we look out for ourselves.

To tell the truth, I believe that young men and women throw off the evil influences of such things more easily than do those of an older generation.

III

THE POWER OF SELF-CONSIOUS memory belongs exclusively to human beings; so far as we can ascertain, animals are entirely without it. Dogs, horses, and other quadrupeds remember individual things when the former environment is repeated; in this kind of memory they often surpass men and women. A horse on a milk route does not need to be directed by his driver; the animal will stop at the right houses and pass the others without hesitation. Furthermore on a black night a horse will find the right road when his rider is utterly lost and bewildered.

Many years ago, accompanied by my Irish setter, I called on a man who lived in a distant part of the city. I had never been there before; and I found the right house only because I had a memorandum of the number. It was in a block of a dozen buildings, all externally alike. I came to the correct address, rang the bell; we were admitted and informed that my friend lived in a room on the second floor. Some months after this, I made a second call, and again I should not have been able to find the house without being able to read the numbers. But the dog, who was running thirty yards ahead, turned in at the right place without hesitation, and the moment the front door was opened, ran upstairs to the proper room.

I mention this, not as a remarkable fact, but as a commonplace illustration of what the average dog can do. I am well aware that stories of an amazing nature could be given, apparently well authenticated, which prove the memory-power of animals. But even taking into account the most extraordinary feats, I do not believe that animals have the gift of self-conscious memory.

The dog remembers the old house, the old face, the old

partridge-cover, when he sees it. But I do not think that the dog, on a winter day, comfortably seated in front of the open fire, says to himself, "That was a wonderful shooting excursion we had last autumn," or, "What a noble dog my father was, and how gladly would I smell him again," or, "What a heavy rain that was yesterday coming home in the automobile!"

Self-conscious memory is like a divine act of creation. It is like divinity, because as physical changes flowed from an act of the divine will, so by the same exercise of power, past events assume reality. Memory is like the creative power of the artist, who puts on a blank canvas a vivid scene. "When to the sessions of sweet silent thought we summon up remembrance of things past," we triumph over space and time, and live with absolute reality away from the body. Thus, by a simple fiat of memory, a man of eighty may be living intensely among the people and the surroundings of his early youth. In the vilest weather we may be conscious only of some lovely summer day. This ability to live keenly away from the body and from the material environment is possibly an earnest of the ability to live after the body has vanished.

> Never the time and the place
> And the loved one all together!
> This path-how soft to pace!
> This May-what magic weather!
> n a dream that loved one's face meets mine,
> But the house is narrow, the place is bleak
> Where, outside, rain and wind combine
> With a furtive ear, if I strive to speak,
> With a hostile eye at my flushing cheek,
> With a malice that marks each word, each sign!
> O enemy sly and serpentine,
> Uncoil thee from the waking man!
> Do I hold the Past
> Thus firm and fast,
> Yet doubt if the Future hold I can?

The inexorable flux of Time can by the creative process of memory be arrested, turned back; the Past once more becomes the Present. Twentytwo years after the death of Schiller, Goethe stood with young Eckermann by the old stone table in the garden at Jena. To Goethe the intervening years vanished and again he sat there with his old friend. He remarked to Eckermann, "You can hardly imagine what a noteworthy place this is. Here Schiller lived. In this garden, on these decaying benches by this old table of stone we used to sit and exchange in conversation many good and memorable words." Then suddenly coming to himself, he said, "That has all gone by. I am myself no longer what I was."

We call on other people to remember when we wish them to do some particular thing, or to follow some particular line of action. Sometimes we make "going-away" presents, so that our bodily absence may not altogether prevent our being remembered. Many persons, writing their last will and testament, will leave some article of jewelry or some thing associated with themselves to a friend, hoping that whenever the friend sees that object, he will remember him who has gone. We try many experiments of this kind, for no one wishes to be entirely forgotten. Doctor Johnson, chronically obsessed by the terror of death, used to quote a certain stanza from Gray's Elegy.

> For who to dumb Forgetfulness a prey,
> This pleasing anxious being e'er resign'd,
> Left the warm precincts of the cheerful day,
> Nor cast one longing, ling'ring look behind?

Many in great pain or in great trouble have called on some one else to remember them. In all human history the most affecting instance of this is the cry of the dying thief, a cry that combined homage, faith, hope, and an appeal for protection. "Lord, remember me when thou comest into thy kingdom."

IV

TOMORROW IS INVARIABLY based on yesterday; no event, no matter how trivial, can be isolated. It belongs in the procession of things, and has its influence. And as not only the deeds, but the thoughts of yesterday become the memories of tomorrow, it is more important to have a well-furnished mind than a bumper crop on the farm or lovely flowers in the garden.

For whilst we are often annoyed by not being able to remember certain things, we are more deeply troubled by not being able to forget. As Prometheus lay chained to the rock while a vulture tore his vitals, so memory may be a ravaging monster tearing our hearts and minds. In Joseph Conrad's first novel, Almayer's Folly, there is a scene so painful as to be almost unendurable. It is where the daughter tells her father she is going away forever, that he will never see her face again. She leaves the house, walks through the sand to-the edge of the water, takes the boat and disappears from view. Then the forsaken father, moving on his hands and knees, carefully obliterates every trace of his daughter's footsteps from the ground; but he cannot take her little feet out of his heart.

It is clear that memory, while it may be a source of joy and delight, may also be a cause of all but unbearable agony. The way to avoid this disaster is by referring once more to the figure of the garden or the bank. If the right deposits are made, the results will be not worthless or tormenting, but full of pleasant fruition. Remorse may, to a large extent, be prevented.

Yet there are times when even the richest memories add to one's poverty I when out of agreeable recollection comes a sharp pain. Tennyson, paraphrasing Dante, said "a sorrow's crown of sorrow is remembering happier things." Housman has expressed the same idea even more poignantly.

Into my heart an air that kills From yon far country blows:
What are those blue remembered hills,
What spires, what farms are those?
That is the land of lost content,
I see it shining plain,
The happy highways where I went,
And cannot come again.

There is, however, an immense difference between the pain of remembrance caused by remorse and that by the remembrance of departed happiness. In the former case we would give anything for the ability to forget; no price would be too great for the complete erasure of this thing from the tablets of the mind. But while the thought of happy experiences may at times make us pensive or even sad, like the memory of lost health in days of sickness, we would not f or all the world have been without those joys.

Indeed a truly healthy and wellbalanced mind will not torment itself with the thought of vanished pleasures; as so many old idiots sigh when they remember their lost youth. The fact that we once had youth and health and happy experiences should give pleasure and not pain to recollection; nobody and nothing can take away those solid enjoyments. It is a selfish or ungrateful or unappreciative mind that makes use of vanished delight only to minister to misery; it is not a clear-sighted way to look at life. "

For, to the true philosopher, lost pleasures do not necessarily mean lost contentment. We lose things out of our lives, lose them irrecoverably, like the agility and freshness of youth, but it is natural to lose them; and if they have contributed to our development, they have well served their purpose.

V

THE EFFECT OF MEMORY on action can hardly be overestimated. In vital or critical moments in our lives we are sometimes saved or inspired by memory. Men who are just about to do something evil suddenly remember a phrase or an incident or a person and are saved from disgrace. Other men in mortal terror, shaking with fear, are by a sudden remembrance made brave. There is no doubt that Captain Scott and his companions, when confronted by a slow and certain death, determined to endure it and not follow out their original plan of suicide, because they remembered their friends at home, their training as Englishmen, the good traditions of their race and breed. And thus every individual deed of heroism becomes a memory, that is, an inspiring and fruitful tradition. Innumerable sailors have played the man because of the example set by Nelson and by Jones. It is impossible to overestimate the productive power of memory.

Also in times of the deepest despondency we are restored to the right frame of mind by a sudden remembrance. "Certain bells, now mute, can jingle," said Browning. We rise from despair by the memory of previous despondencies from which we emerged safely or over which we triumphed. When Christian and Hopeful were in the dungeon of Giant

Despair, and were advised by the Giant to commit suicide, the following conversation too'. place.

At this they trembled greatly, and I think that Christian fell into a Swound; but coming a little to himself again, they renewed their discourse about the Giant's counsel; and whether yet they had best to take it or no. Now Christian again seemed to be for doing it, but Hopeful made his second reply as followeth.

My Brother, said he, remembrest thou not how valiant thou

hast been heretofore. Apollyon could not crush thee, nor could all that thou didst hear, or see, or feel in the Valley of the Shadow o f Death. . . .

Well, on Saturday about midnight they began to pray, and continued in Prayer till almost break of day.

Now a little before it was day, good Christian, as one half amazed, brake out in this passionate Speech, What a fool, quoth he, ant I that to lie in a stinking Dungeon, when I may as well be at liberty! I have a Key in my bosom, called Promise, that will, I am persuaded, open any Lock in Doubting Castle. Then said Hopeful, That's good news; good Brother pluck it out of thy bosom and try.

Sometimes under stress, if we cannot remember any particular act of heroism, or any particular emergency from which we have previously escaped, it may be well if we can remember simply that we are men, not

beasts; and that accordingly we should act like men, and not lower the standard of humanity.

Fathers and mothers are often depressed by the apparent indifference of their children to their admonitions and even to their example. It is well therefore to observe that the good influence of parents on children is much greater after the parents are dead than when they were alive. It is only natural for boys and girls to rebel against the advice or commands of their parents. "Father and mother of course are good people, but they don't know life as it is now; they are not familiar with the facts." Yet long after the older ones are dead, they reach out hands from the grave and guide their offspring. As the faces of men in maturity progressively resemble their parents, so and even more so do their conduct, their speeches, and their thoughts. Good precepts and good examples, though at the time they seem not to make the slightest impression, are not lost; no good word or good action is ever lost. They bear fruit in later years.

A distinguished professor of science remarked, "When I was young I disagreed with everything my father and mother told me. I believed exactly the contrary, and was sure I was right. Now I am an old man, and I know that what they said was true."

Perhaps of all the innumerable illustrations of the power of remembrance in spiritual development, the most dramatic and the most effective is a simple sentence spoken by Our Lord at a little supper with his disciples.

This do in remembrance of me. It is strange and startling that not one of the famous formal banquets that have taken place on state occasions in history, has had one millionth part of the influence on mankind effected by this meagre repast, taken in obscurity by a few peasants and fishermen. Think of the great occasions in the history of the world when state banquets were held and royalty graced the board-when decisions of war were taken, whole countries parcelled out! How brief their influence, how transitory their plans and projects discussed with such pomp and arrogance!

Even in the twentieth century, when some measure of great importance is to be launched, it usually begins with a well-advertised banquet. And today, if a public dinner should be arranged at which the participants should be the President of the United States, the Prime Minister of Great Britain, the Dictator of Italy, the leading Representatives in power and diplomacy of all the countries of the world, Plenipotentiaries to settle the future of international relations-this banquet would in its influence be negligible in comparison with the simple repast held in that little room, where, as the bread and wine were taken, an obscure individual said, "This do in remembrance of me." For today in every part of the world, men and women partake of the bread and wine, and remember.

www.ingramcontent.com/pod-product-compliance
Lightning Source LLC
Chambersburg PA
CBHW021950040426
42448CB00008B/1335